HOW TO FOCUS

54 Habits, Tools and Ideas to Create Superhuman Focus, Eliminate Distractions, Stop Procrastination and Achieve More With Less Work

A.V. Mendez

TABLE OF CONTENTS

Introduction ... *page 4*
1 - The Pomodoro Technique ... *page 7*
2 - The "No Device" Principle ... *page 10*
3 - Set a Daily Task ... *page 13*
4 - Meditation Works ... *page 16*
5 - Use a Calendar App ... *page 19*
6 - Teach People to Set an Appointment ... *page 22*
7 - Time Chunking ... *page 25*
8 - Use the Right Background Music ... *page 28*
9 - Find "Your" Location ... *page 31*
10 - Create a To-Do List ... *page 34*
11 - The Lighting Matters ... *page 37*
12 - Stop Multitasking ... *page 39*
13 - Do Your Most Important Task First ... *page 42*
14 - Visual Reminders ... *page 45*
15 - Build Your Willpower ... *page 47*
16 - Work Chunking (The Secret to Getting Started) ... *page 50*
17 - Batch Similar Tasks ... *page 53*
18 - Set a Due Date ... *page 55*
19 - Prepare Your Digital Workload ... *page 58*
20 - Declutter Your Digital Workload ... *page 60*
21 - Declutter Your Work Environment ... *page 63*
22 - Get Help ... *page 66*
23 - Turn Your Notifications Off ... *page 69*
24 - Use a Noise Cancelling Headphone ... *page 72*
25 - Drink a Green Juice First Thing in the Morning ... *page 74*
26 - Should You Avoid Caffeine? ... *page 76*
27 - Preserve Your Emotional Energy ... *page 79*
28 - Say No and Mean It ... *page 82*
29 - Say Yes, But Only If It Matches Your Goals ... *page 85*
30 - Exercise Every day ... *page 87*
31 - Take Short Walks ... *page 90*
32 - Run, Run, Run ... *page 92*
33 - Sleep Soundly ... *page 94*

34 - Take Short Breaks ... *page 97*

35 - Start and Follow a Routine ... *page 99*

36 - Take Naps ... *page 101*

37 - Stretch Yourself – Part 1 ... *page 103*

38 - Stretch Yourself – Part 2 ... *page 105*

39 – Note Taking Apps? ... *page 107*

40 - Review Your Day ... *page 109*

41 - Review Your Week ... *page 111*

42 - Review Your Month and Year ... *page 113*

43 - Do Not Be a Perfectionist ... *page 115*

44 - Schedule Your "Pleasure Time" ... *page 120*

45 - Learn to Disconnect ... *page 123*

46 - Avoid Your Email ... *page 125*

47 - Ask What the Process Requires ... *page 127*

48 - Work with Two Computer Monitors ... *page 130*

49 - Mindmap Your Ideas ... *page 132*

50 - Increase Your Attention Span ... *page 134*

51 - The Do Not Disturb Sign ... *page 136*

52 - Create a "NOT TO-DO" List ... *page 137*

53 - Ditch the Open Door Policy ... *page 139*

54 - Be Genuinely Interested in What You Do ... *page 140*

Conclusion ... *page 141*

A Special Request ... *page 142*

Other Books ... *page 143*

Introduction

Focus is a currency that is hard to get nowadays because we live in a world full of distractions.

So, what can we do about it?

How can we achieve maximum focus?

How can we make sure that we don't waste our time?

The answer is to build habits and follow ideas that help us eliminate distractions. The answer is to set ourselves up for success by changing our mindset and by building a tougher resistance to distractions. The answer is to combine different ideas for us to maximize our results.

Are you ready? Let's get started.

P.S. This book is *as straight to the point type of book as you can get*. I don't make it longer just to earn more money from Amazon. I make it as long and as short as necessary. My goal is not to give you hundreds of pages of useless information. My goal is to get you to take action one day at a time. I hope that the book's structure lends itself to doing just that.

HOW TO FOCUS

This book will give you 54 ideas that you can implement one by one so you can increase your ability to focus. Each idea includes an *Action Guide* that serves as the main lesson that you can apply to maximize the learnings and turn them into something concrete. You don't have to do all of them but I highly recommend that you try as much of the ideas as possible. They're all easy-to-implement mini-lessons that when added up, leads to a more focused way of life. Good luck and let's get this thing going!

1 - The Pomodoro Technique

The Pomodoro technique changed my life. Before *the Pomodoro,* I waste 30-45 minutes every day before I start working!

After implementing the Pomodoro, my habits changed and I was able to focus immediately on my work.

The Pomodoro forces my butt to take action.

The Pomodoro is basically about working in time chunks.

It's usually 25 minutes of work, then 5 minutes of rest.

Then you work again for 25 minutes and then rest for 10-15 minutes.

And then you just repeat the process over and over again until you finish your chosen task.

I use either tomatotimers.com (free) or a physical tomato timer.

I recommend that you focus on only one type of task per 1 Pomodoro cycle. This helps you focus your mind and not let it wander everywhere.

You can also use the method in any task that you want. You can use it for writing, managing your employees, meetings, chatting with customers, and even napping!

I also recommend that you use it on your hardest tasks. For example, if you're a content creator, then the hardest part of your task is creating content every day.

Go test the Pomodoro method and follow the 25/5/25/10-15 workflow.

There's a reason why every productivity coach out there teaches this method.

Simply put, **it works**.

Fun Fact: I almost didn't put this idea just because I know that every book out there about focus and productivity already discussed this method. But I realize that I will be doing a huge disservice for those people who may have never heard of it.

Go use it, it works!

Acton Guide:

Identify your most important task of the day and apply the Pomodoro Technique. Use www.tomatotimers.com (I'm not getting paid to promote this) or buy a physical timer on Amazon or your local shop.

2 - The "No Device" Principle

This one is hard to implement but is already something necessary to do.

Unless you really need a device in your desk to finish the work you are doing, I highly recommend that you put your mobile phones, iPads, and any other device in another room.

The harder for you to grab your device, the more unlikely it is for you to use it.

This will save you so much time and energy that you'll be able to finally focus more on the things that you want to do.

This is more of a habit than willpower.

Before you start your work, go ahead and put your devices on places that are hard to reach. If you're in the office, put your phone on your locker or below your desk.

Also, put them into silent mode as well.

Make this a habit and watch your focus increase by at least 2 folds! Guaranteed!

Action Guide:

What are the devices you have that only serves as a distraction every time you do your work?

Ask yourself, do you really need that device to achieve the goals you set for yourself that day? Or is it just something that you put beside you because it's a *habit*?

Most likely, it's just a bad habit that you developed over the years. Well, now it's time to let go of that destructive habit.

It's time to finally take control of your own agenda.

Identify these devices and then put them away.

You'll be doing yourself a big favor. Your productivity and ability to focus will increase, and you'll start to wonder how much time you could've saved if you only applied this technique years ago.

Don't be guilty though... Just apply what you learned and start today!

3 - Set a Daily Task

Even before the day starts, I always already know what things I should be working on for the day.

How?

The night before, I always create a list of *daily tasks* that I will do for the next day.

I start by making a list of the most important tasks that will have a big effect on my goal.

Next, I prioritize my task from *most important to less important*.

Then I make sure that I only have a maximum of 3 tasks per day. Too much on the list can demotivate us. Also, we tend to underestimate the time we need in order to finish a specific project. Limiting your tasks to 3 will give you more flexibility in finishing all your projects for the day.

Let's say that I'm an online guitar teacher.

My daily tasks could be the following:

1 - Creating guitar tutorials

2 - Editing the videos

3 - Posting videos on YouTube

4 - Creating online courses

5 - Marketing online courses

6 - Customer service

7 - Administrative tasks

8 - Financial planning for the business

9 - Advertising management

As you can see here, doing all of these in one day is impossible especially if you're a *one-man business*. So, you have to identify which tasks you should be doing every day.

Most likely, it'll be guitar tutorials and product marketing.

So, start your day with the creation part and then use the other half of your day on marketing. Then on other days, you can focus on creating online courses content and managing your advertisements.

You don't have to do everything in one day.

Put your focus on 2 tasks and then add more if you still have lots of extra time.

Action Guide:

Make a list of the tasks that will have a huge effect on your goal. Out of all those tasks, what are the top 3 most important stuff? What are the *must-do*? What are the things that have a direct impact on your goals? Do them first and then add other other things if you still have time to spare.

4 - Meditation Works

A lot of people misunderstands this word. They think that meditation is only about being silent and doing nothing, trying to achieve *nirvana*.

We have too many thoughts and these things distract us every day. Meditation is about calming your mind.

It's been proven to lower our stress levels and helps us think clearly.

So how do you do meditation if you're easily distracted?

The answer is you start small.

Instead of going for 30 minutes of silence, you can start with 2 minutes.

Here's what I personally do:

I put in an earplug so I can have silence. Then I shut the lights off, set a 2-minute timer and then go to the corner of my room.

I breathe in for 3 seconds, and I breathe out for another 3.
I listen to my breath. I don't try to not think about anything.

I just imagine my breath going from my nose to my tummy and then vice versa.

This simple way of meditation is what helped me fight that initial resistance to meditate.
After 1 week of doing this, I increased my meditation time to 5 minutes… and then ten….
I'm up to the point that I do it now in 15-20 minutes per day.

I don't know the exact science behind it. All I know is that it helped me focus more, sleep better and be less irritable.

I'm more patient now compared to before I started meditating. And as woo-woo as this sound, life is just more peaceful for me.

Maybe I did achieve nirvana. Maybe it's my own definition of nirvana. Peace, quiet, calm and patience.

Action Guide:

Start small if you must. If you have never tried meditation in your entire life, then start by doing it in your own chair. Do this now… Close your eyes, put your hands beside you, then breathe in and breathe out for 3 seconds each. Repeat the cycle 5 times and then open your eyes when you're done.

That's it. That's how you get started with meditation. No need to buy apps or any meditation devices for now.

Once you've done the exercise, increase your breathing cycle to 10.

Go make it a process. You don't have to do it all in one day.

5 - Use a Calendar App

Truth be told, I've never been a calendar app guy.

But when I went into sales, I realized how important they can be. Sure, not every job needs it, but if you can maximize its use, then it'll help you become more productive and it'll help you to be more focused on the right things.

So how do you use a calendar app?

To-Do List

You can put your to-do list on your calendar app. This helps you in streamlining the process. You can input one task and include the time frame needed for you to finish that certain task.

Appointment List

Another thing you can use it for is by setting appointments or meetings.

Since you can connect your Desktop app to your mobile app, you can easily look at your schedule and instantly know whether you have an appointment or not.

This also assures that you won't miss any meetings or client appointments just because you *forgot about it.* This is an unacceptable reason so make sure that this won't happen to you.

For Mac, I usually just use my stock Calendar app included in the laptop itself. You can also connect this to your iPhone's calendar app.
For PC users, I recommend that you use Google Calendar. You can then connect it to your Google Calendar App which you can download whether you're using iOS or Android.

Action Guide:

Choose a calendar app that works for you.

You can start with the basics:

For Mac and iOS (iPhone, iPad,) - Calendar App for Mac/Calendar App for iOS

For PC/Other Laptops - Google Calendar for PC/Google Calendar for iOS or Android

Check out these links for some of the best apps that experts are using and recommending:

https://www.slant.co/topics/855/~best-calendar-apps-for-android

https://www.tomsguide.com/us/pictures-story/442-best-calendar-apps.html

Some of them are paid and some are free.

If you're only getting started, just start with free. Then upgrade as your needs increase.

6 - Teach People to Set an Appointment

Time Vampires.

That's what you get when people do not respect the value of your time. You have people texting, emailing, messaging, and going to your office door saying "let's talk, it'll only take a minute."

And of course, it's always never *just a minute.*

You see, these time vampires are everywhere! So, you have to guard your time like a Doberman guards its owner's house.

What I do is I teach people to set appointments.

If someone texts me, and it's not urgent, I always answer on a specific time frame (5pm-5:30pm). My phone is always on silent and has an automatic voice message that says I don't answer calls. I ask them to text me and I'll call them myself if it's an urgent matter. I make sure to stress that I don't reply to messages or calls because it affects my productivity.

It's the same with Facebook messenger. I only check it once every 2 days and honestly, I never had an urgent message on Facebook. It's always people asking for something. It's more of *can you do this for me? Can you send this? Here's a generic question, can you give an answer to this?* I just "seen" messages and don't reply unless I really needed to.

Another time vampire are meetings! OMG. Please, you don't need to run daily meetings! Unless you're in sales, then it's not needed. What I do is I tell my staff that all our meetings will be done standing up. Guess what? Some kind of magic happened. Our meetings are all finished within 5-15 minutes. This saved me an extra 1-2 hours a day doing something more productive.

Action Guide:

Identify who are the time vampires in your life.

Where do they come from? *Facebook? Meetings? The "got a minute?" people in the office?*

Then teach them to set an appointment or to relay their message on hours that you're not busy working on your "must do" tasks.

This will save you so much time you'll wonder why you haven't implemented this before in your life.

7 - Time Chunking

Time chunking is scheduling your work hours in time chunks. So instead of working 2 hours straight, we can do something like this:

0:00 - 45:00 - Work
45:00 - 55:00 - Rest
55:00 - 1:30 - Work
1:30 - 1:40 - Rest
1:30 - 2:00 - Work

This helps you manage and maintain your energy. If you work on a very demanding job, then this will help you in keeping your productivity levels high throughout the day.

The difference between Pomodoro and Time-Chunking (TC) is that Pomodoro is just a Time Chunking Technique. TC is the foundation, Pomodoro is the implementation.

So how can you do TC the most effective way?

The key is to test what works for you.

For some, the Pomodoro time-frame works for them. 25 minutes of work, 5 minutes of rest, then repeat the process.

However, for people who lacked focus and attention, then you probably need more than 25 minutes (so you can sort yourself out first). I suggest starting with 50 minutes of work and then 10 minutes rest.

And yes, you do need to rest. In fact, it's the main secret why time-chunking works. Our body and brain needs the rest. There's just no way we can perform on a daily basis without taking a break. It's impossible to do it long-term.

Also, as your work day goes by, the more rest you need to schedule.

If you've already scheduled 5 cycles of *50 minutes of work and 10 minutes of rest* in the morning, then change it to *35 minutes of work, and 5–10 minutes of rest cycle* in the afternoon.

This will help you maintain your productivity level while still being effective at what you do. The goal is obviously not just being productive. It's also about producing the best outcome you can do.

Action Guide:

Use the time-chunking method on your next task. If you're easily distracted and needs time to adjust before working, then schedule a 50-minute time-chunk for work and 10 minutes for rest.

The first 10 minutes will be the hardest. It's the resistance phase of the game. You'll fumble, go to FB, Twitter, YouTube, and every other website just to avoid work. Give yourself permission to fail in your first few tries of the TC method.

Don't judge yourself too early in the game. Eventually, you'll learn to let go of the distractions and learn to just *do the work*.

8 - Use the Right Background Music

Listening to music has been proven to make us calmer and makes us more productive.

However, there is no one-size fits all type of music.

One type of music may calm you but the same music may make me anxious. The best that I can do is show you what works for me and some of my staff in the office.

Classical Music

For creative tasks, listening to Mozart and Beethoven works best. I don't know what's in their music, but it makes you think clearly and it helps in letting the ideas fly.

White Noise

We're creatures of nature. For millions of years, we evolved with lots of noises in the background. The trees, the birds, the animals, the breeze of the air, etc. So, it's no surprise to me that lots of people recommend working with white noise in the background as it makes them feel calmer and more "in tuned" with the nature.

Music Loop

For some, listening to the same music until it fades into the background becomes their shield against the world. The music loop becomes the background, and you start to put them on the side of your subconscious, allowing you to focus on the main task.

Favorite Spotify Playlists

I've asked a lot of people and random music from Spotify works best when they are doing administrative tasks. My theory is when you're listening to your favorite music, the admin tasks (which can be boring) becomes really exciting to do.

Action Guide:

I recommend starting with classical music. It's the safest choice and it's something that works for almost everyone. It doesn't matter what your job is. It's always a pleasure to listen to Mozart no matter what the situation is. Just don't use the same music when you're trying to get to sleep.

Check out this article to find the best classical music for focusing on your work.

https://www.independent.co.uk/student/student-life/Studies/classical-music-and-studying-the-top-10-pieces-to-listen-to-for-exam-success-a7037841.html

9 - Find "Your" Location

Your work location can also have a big impact on how focus you can be.

Some people swear that the natural noise from coffee shops works for them. Some people like to feel the vibe of having a co-working space. Then for some (like me), we prefer the space in the corner of the room.

Coffee Shop

If you'll work at a coffee shop, then expect it to be noisy. Expect that there will be more distractions. *That pretty girl in front of you drinking her chocolate frappe. That guy on his iPhone playing pubg. Or the sound of the coffee machine grinding all those gears to make you the best coffee possible.*

So, make sure that you're adept to working in this kind of environment.

Also, you can use coffee shops as your alternative office for doing administrative tasks. Think of it this way. The office is for production, and the coffee shops are for management.

Co-working Space

Another one that can get noisy at times is co-working spaces. If you work at home and you're already bored of always working alone, then you can feed with the energy of other people who's *just like you*. Lots of people in co-working spaces are startups or self-employed freelancers who can choose to work at home if they want to.

Office Space

If you're an employee, then you'll have fewer options where you can work. 90% of the time, you will be working in the company office. This is where time vampires hang-out a lot! So just be wary of who you talk to on a daily basis. Everyone's out there with their own agendas. Make sure that you're guarding yours like a kid guarding her candies.

Your Own Room

This works for me whenever I'm writing. I just can't do it in the office when there's a handful of people, who at any time can distract my workflow. I recommend this to anyone working on a creative task like writing, painting, coming up with ideas, and planning in general.

Action Guide:

Find a location that fits your task. Most creative endeavors require silence, while management stuff can still thrive in chaos.

10 - Create a To-Do List

To-do list has gotten a bad rap lately. I keep seeing lots of people on my Facebook feed saying that to-do lists are for average people. LOL.

The problem is not in the to-do list itself, it's in the way people create and implement their to-do lists.

If you're a lazy person and you have a list of 10 things to do per day, then your to-do list will not work!

I recommend no more than 7 of specific things to do every day.

Also, in case you're wondering, the difference between a to-do list and a daily task is that a to-do list is more specific.

A daily task may be this: write my book

A to-do list may look like this: write 1,000 words in 1 hour - (9am-10am)

It's more specific and it is time-bounded at the same time.

HOW TO CREATE A TO-DO LIST THAT WORKS.

1 - Start with the most important stuff. *If you're a real estate agent, then your most important task is to get clients.*

2 - Create a specific list of 3 things to do in the morning and 3-4 in the afternoon. The first 3 should be the most important and urgent tasks. If you're just getting started with to-do lists, then only put 2 tasks in the morning and another 2 in the afternoon.

3 - Track your to-do list every day. *How many hours does it take to finish certain tasks?* You should know these things so you can create the correct time-frame for finishing them on your future to-do lists.

Action Guide:

Start creating a to-do list and only put a
maximum of 4 things to do in the beginning. Too
many tasks will make you feel overwhelmed,
which may lead you to not take action in the first
place.

Follow the 3-step process above to get started.

11 - The Lighting Matters

The room's lighting affects the ambiance of your workplace.

Too much light and it'll be almost distracting, too little and you'll start to feel like you're working with your eyes closed.

There are also some rooms with yellow lights in them (I hate those lights).

My recommendation is that you use a white Philips type of bulb. Bright enough that you can see what you're working on but not too much, that it's already affecting the reflection on your screen.

This is a simple tweak, but effective nonetheless in improving your focus.

Action Guide:

Check this website out to find the best type of light for you.

http://www.lighting.philips.com/main/prof/led-lamps-and-tubes/led-bulbs/sceneswitch-ledbulbs

Email their customer service if you have some important questions to ask.

12 - Stop Multitasking

It seems like there's a never-ending debate whether multitasking works or not.

Here's the truth. IT DOES WORK. But not in a positive way.

Sure, you can do 2 things at a time. But you'll never be as effective as you do when you focus on just 1 thing at a time.

This isn't even a debate anymore. Multitasking just plain sucks when it comes to maximizing our effectiveness.

We only think that it's working because we're finishing 2 tasks.

But the truth is, we can finish those 2 jobs faster and more effectively if we only do them one at a time.

The problem lies in our ability to re-focus.

When you do 2 things, your brain needs to adjust to the other task before it can completely recalibrate.

Don't believe me? Go do your main task for 20 minutes straight and then go watch YouTube for 10 minutes. I guarantee you that there's a good chance that you won't be as focused as you when you return to your original task. Your brain is in work mode and then you put entertainment time in there. The brain gets confused and now, it needs the time to re-adjust to your new mindset.

So, stop multitasking!
It works in making you feel like you're getting things done.

But it's an illusion. Focusing on one task at a time makes you more effective and efficient.

Multitasking makes your brain confused and it lets you wander off, thus making you waste precious time that you could've used on a more productive manner.

Action Guide:

Whenever you caught yourself multitasking, stop, close your eyes and breathe in and out 3 times. Then stop doing the other task or close the tabs that are not needed on your main task. Fight the urge to open social media sites or any blogging or news websites.

If you're writing, then write. Don't open YouTube and watch the highlights of your favorite team. Schedule that for later instead!

If you're calling prospects, then call and do nothing else! Don't start planning for lunch or stop cleaning your desk. Focus on understanding what your prospect is saying.

Stop multitasking. Stop multitasking. Stop multitasking.

I hope I'm clear about that. :P

13 - Do Your Most Important Task First

The reason why I stress doing the most important task first thing in the morning, is that I understand the way our mind and body works.

Mornings are when we have the most energy. Lunch and beyond is just a bonus in my book.

So how you identify your most important tasks?

First, you have to know your goal.

What do you want to achieve? If you're a songwriter, then the most important activity in your day will be songwriting.

In this case, you must spend the first 2-3 hours of your day writing songs.

Remember this. **Morning is for creating, and the afternoon is for marketing and management.** This applies to a lot of jobs out there.

Obviously, this may be different for some.

Let's say that your job is an English teacher. And let's say that your main task is *to teach Asian executives how to speak proper English*. If possible, try to schedule your sessions in the morning. Then use the afternoon for getting referrals and marketing your services. If you're just starting out and you don't have clients yet, then you can do this in vice versa. Focus on getting clients in the morning, then do your teaching sessions in the afternoon.

Action Guide:

Identify your most important task.

This is the task that will bring in the results that you want to get. What's important to you doesn't have to mean, that it's also the most important to someone with the same job that you have. Your goals and your progress in the field might be different, so your priorities will be different as well.

So, you can't just compare what you do to what others in your field does.

Find your own "*main task of the day*" and start doing them in the mornings.

14 - Visual Reminders

These are physical and digital reminders of things to be focusing on.

They don't have to be the tasks you should be doing (although you can certainly do that). You can add motivational quotes or pictures that inspire you to focus and go back to taking action.

They could be in the form of printed pictures, sticky notes, refrigerator magnets, and notes on your computer.

Action Guide:

Create your own visual reminders to maximize motivation and focus.

If you're having trouble remembering your daily tasks, then write it on a sticky note and post in your computer or your desk.

You can also put words of encouragement around you by posting printed motivational quotes.

These are just things that remind you to keep going.

This is a simple trick that gives me that extra boost to keep on working and to avoid my usual distractions.

15 - Build Your Willpower

Although it's never a good idea to only rely on your willpower, it does help to have some of it.

I think it's most important when you're just in the process of starting something.

You need that initial boost of willpower that will take you from procrastinating and being all over the place, to finally doing the task you're supposed to be doing.

So how do you build your willpower?

Well, you feed it.

You do it be fighting the resistance.

Let's say that your main task for the day is to call your prospects. Willpower thrives by feeding action into it.

What you can do is to start looking at the task as if it is a puzzle. You finish it piece by piece...

So, if you're calling a prospect to sell something, here's what it would look like:

First, you grab the phone... that's it. That's your first goal.

Now you have a piece of the puzzle and you just added a tiny amount of willpower in you.
Next, you hold the phone and put it in your ear. That's another step. Then you dial. Then you start talking... and so on.

This may seem like a ridiculous way to look at it, but the strategy just flat out works! They say that the pros don't need willpower to take action. They just need discipline to actually do the work.

But we're all not "pros" here... at least not yet.

So it's still nice to have some willpower that can take you over the hump of starting out.

Action Guide:

Start building your willpower by feeding it with small actions. This brings positive reinforcement and your brain starts to remember all these small wins and how it makes you feel. This adds to your willpower, thus making it stronger over time.

The more you feed it, the stronger it becomes.

The more you take action, the more your willpower becomes a strength of yours, ready to back you up and help you achieve maximum focus.

16 - Work Chunking (The Secret to Getting Started)

One of the hardest parts of getting things done is trying to start a project. The harder the task is, the harder it is to get started.

What we can do is apply the work-chunking method so we can fight the initial resistance of starting a project.

It's the same concept from the last idea I showed you. But this time, we'll take it to the next level by giving you more examples of how to do it.

Okay, say you're a copywriter and you were asked to create a sales page. The only problem is you're not in the mood to take action and you'd rather sleep all day… also, the deadline is in 3 days.

So how do you focus on your work and how do you even start?

This is where work-chunking comes in.

We can break-down the task that we're about to do, and implement small actions that lead to us finishing our task.

In our example, it's about creating a sales page.

A sales page has many parts but the basics are headlines, introduction, benefits via bullet form, product information, and call to action.

Instead of thinking "sales page" as a whole, we can trick our brain to focus on the headline first. Just say it "I'll **only** do the headline."

Then you start coming up with ideas for the headline. Next, you'll say "I'll only do the introduction"... then you come up with an introduction... then you just repeat the process over and over again.

It's about focusing on the steps within your chosen task, one idea at a time.

Action Guide:

Think about the tasks that you do on a daily basis. Ask how can you apply the work-chunking method on all of these tasks?

Break down the steps needed on every task, and set a time frame for finishing each step if possible.

Work-chunking is powerful; you just have to use it the right way.

17 - Batch Similar Tasks

One of the ways to avoid getting overwhelmed by things to do is to batch similar tasks. On our daily tasks, we tend to do 3-4 different categories depending on the job that you have.

These 4 categories are Creation, Management, Marketing, and Administrative.

Batching the tasks creates less confusion and it streamlines the process for getting things done.

I recommend that you do anything related to Creation in the morning. Tasks like creating content, writing, creating your product, etc.

After the creation part, you can either do the management or the marketing part. And the last category you can focus on is the administrative part of the business.

If you already have employees, then this can all be done simultaneously. However, I still recommend that you focus on the creation or production part first thing in the morning.

Action Guide:

Make a list of all the things that you or your business does on a daily basis. Just create a mindmap and dump all the information.

Next, create 4 columns on an excel file and categorize all the tasks via Creation, Management, Marketing or Administrative.
I guarantee you that you'll help streamline the process, and you'll gain more clarity in what tasks you or your business should really be doing every day.

18 - Set a Due Date/Deadline

All of the things I do related to my business has due dates or deadlines. Why? Simply because it's an effective way to save time and to make sure that we're actually getting things done.

If the tasks that you do doesn't have a deadline, then it's probably not important enough to do now!

The problem with some of the to-do lists that people create is they do not put a deadline so they end up not doing the to-do list in the first place.

I don't care of it's just a "quick task." Define what quick is because time is relative to the task. 30 minutes might be quick for some but someone else may see it as too slow.

So set deadlines and make sure that you're following a strict rule of finishing in those deadlines. If you found that your deadlines are too fast for you to handle, then simply change the deadline on your next (but the same type of) project.

Assessing Time-Frame

The bigger the goal, the further away the deadline will be. Some goals need 2 years and some needs 2 months.

Track your progress and evaluate if you're moving in the right direction. Remember, you can always pivot in the right way, but the first step in doing that is realizing that you are moving in the wrong direction. I can't stress this enough, always re-evaluate your situation and goals, and make sure that you're moving to and not further from the goal.

Action Guide:

Look at the main goals that you have. Assess the situation and be honest at what you'll find. Are you moving forward or backward? Pivot if you must. Then start setting hard deadlines.

These are not just *deadlines for show*. These are deadlines that you would actually want to beat. There will be long-term deadlines and there will be short ones. The way to beat the long-term ones is by making sure that your daily and weekly due dates are getting beat as well.

19 - Prepare Your Digital Workload

I always prepare all the tools that I need **the night before the workday.** I work on my computer so what I do is I open all the tabs that I need for my work and pin them through the Google Chrome Tab Pin function.

I also open all the folders, word file or any application that is needed for me to finish my most important tasks.

Anything that I don't need is strictly not to be opened.

I also hide all the files on my desktop for the time being, so I don't get distracted and open random stuff on my computer.

Doing this helps you set yourself up for success.

If all the tools that you need are already there, it is more likely for you to start taking action, instead of fumbling around wasting your time on nonsense stuff.

Action Guide:

Identify the tasks that you need to do tomorrow.

Next, identify the tools you need in order to finish those tasks.

30-60 minutes before you sleep, open your computer and open the tabs (pin them), applications and other digital tools that you need in order to successfully finish your *to-do* list.

20 - Declutter Your Digital Workload

Another way to help you focus on your tasks is to declutter your digital workload.

There are so many things that you can do that will help your ability to focus, these are the most important ones I personally did:

1 - Email subscription

I recommend unsubscribing to most of the emails you receive. Trust me, you don't need that coupon to buy a jerky beef, you don't need to follow 10 internet marketing gurus to learn Facebook ads, and you certainly don't need TMZ sending you "breaking news" about some idiot celebrity.

Add all these subscriptions up and you'll quickly realize how much time you're wasting on other people's agenda. These are digital time-vampires! Avoid them as much as you can.

2 - Desktop Apps

Another thing you can do is to delete some apps that you're not using anymore. They only serve as possible distractions for you. Plus, the constant *update this app* notification can also waste your energy you could've used on being productive.

Next, arrange your desktop apps by function. Put the word, excel and PowerPoint apps together. Then put all your editing apps together as well - stuff like photoshop, Camtasia, etc.

If they fit in one category, put them close to each other so you can easily find them when you're about to use them.

3 - Arrange Folders

This one is a biggie, and you probably need to take half a day to a whole day of free time to manage your folder and files.

What you can do is create a folder for videos, word files, images, and projects.

4 - Minimize Social Media Usage

Spending time on social media, especially if it's not work-related, is a waste of time. There's just no other way to describe it. It's a waste of time and it's stupid.

I recommend only using Facebook, Twitter, Instagram, and YouTube once every 2 days. Schedule your social media time if you have to. 20-30 minutes for each app is plenty.

Action Guide:

Schedule your "digital declutter work day" and choose one or two you can fix on that day. You can start with e-mail since it's the easiest thing to do. Check out this link to know more about finding and unsubscribing to most of your subscriptions.

https://www.pcworld.com/article/3181014/3-tools-for-easily-unsubscribing-to-emails.html

21 - Declutter Your Work Environment

Now it's time to focus on your physical environment. For years, I refused to clean my home-office on a daily basis. I reasoned that "I'm just a messy guy, that's who I am."

I didn't know at that time, but looking back, it's crazy how it affected my productivity. There's literally just stuff everywhere.

Papers, books, pens, water bottles, unwashed clothes, probably snakes (lol)...ugh, it's disgusting even to think about it now.

I didn't realize how it affected by mentality. Now, it's clear to me that having stuff everywhere really messes up with your flow. It's like there's distraction everywhere I look at.

But once I started to clean up my room (thanks Jordan Peterson), I became more productive, focused, less irritable and less prone to distractions.

It's honestly a whole new world for me! I'm not sure if you can relate, but maybe to a degree, you do.

I recommend that you declutter your work environment.

This will give you more focus and probably even less anxiety.

Start with the ones that you don't use. Throw them away or hide them on a room that you do not use.

Also, if you can't do it on your own, then hire a "Marie Kondo" type of professional who can help you manage your declutter.

Action Guide:

Schedule one-day off from work (or do it on weekends) and start decluttering your work environment.

If you work at home, then you probably need half a day to 3 days to finish it. However, if you work in an office, less than a day is more than enough.

Start with your desk. Throw away everything you do not need or give them away to an officemate.

Next, focus on paper works. Hide what you don't use anymore. 90% of the papers you have are probably useless now. Take the time to make sure that you actually don't need them anymore before you start shredding them.

22 - Use a Noise Cancelling Headphone

I work best when I'm at peace. I hate outside noise and I really can't stand being distracted.

I can be productive for 30 minute straight, and as soon as one guy comes over me and ask for something, I immediately turn into this unproductive mess of a person. For some reason, it'll take me up to 30 minutes again to gain back that lost focus.

So one day I decided to buy noise-canceling headphones.
It has two main benefits for me.

1 - I don't get to hear outside noises.

This is a big one for me. I'm easily distracted and I get irritable pretty fast. Not hearing other people's B.S. is worth its weight in gold for me.

2 - People stopped bothering me.

There's something about having a big headphone on your ear, people notice it and they're more likely not to bother you or talk to you. This saved me so much focus energy that I'd pay 10x the amount I paid for my noise-canceling headphone if I have to. It's just so worth it.

Alternatively, you can buy earplugs if you're working alone from home and you don't have as much distraction from other people.

Action Guide:

Go to your nearest store and look for a noise canceling headphone. It doesn't have to be ultra-expensive.

Also, you can search for best noise canceling headphones on Google and buy yours on Amazon.

I personally wouldn't pay more than $300 for one.

Here are some of the models you can look at:

1 - SONY WH-1000XM3 - $320
2 - BOWERS & WILKINS PX - $320
3 - BEATS STUDIO3 WIRELESS - $250
4 - SONY WH-1000XM2 - $350

Read the whole review here: https://www.t3.com/features/best-noise-cancelling-headphones

23 - Turn Your Notifications Off

You don't need the notification.

Repeat after me… "I DON'T NEED THE NOTIFICATION."

It'll only serve as distractions instead of reminders, and you know it too! So let's just go straight into taking care of this problem.

MAC

1. On your Mac, choose Apple menu > System Preferences, then click Notifications.
2. Select News in the list on the left, then set options on the right. To stop all notifications, click None. For more information about the options, click the Help button in the corner of the pane.

PC

1. On your computer, open Chrome.
2. At the top right, click More Settings.

3.At the bottom, click Advanced.

4.Under "Privacy and security," click Content settings.

5.Click Notifications.

6.Choose to block or allow notifications: Block all: Turn off Ask before sending.

iOS

1.Launch the Settings app on your iPhone or iPad.

2.Tap Notifications.

3.Select the app for which you want to turn on or off banners.

4.Toggle the Allow Notifications switch on if it's not already.

5.Tap Banners to enable or disable them.

Android

1.Go to Settings > Sound and Notification > App Notifications.

2.Tap the app you want to stop.

3.Tap the toggle for Block, which will never show notifications from this app.

Action Guide:

Choose the device that you have and follow the instructions above. I got them directly from their respective authority websites so it should work.

Remember, you can choose to turn on a specific app if you really need a notification for that application.

24 - Get Help

Not all of the tasks that we'll put on our to-do list are possible to be finished by us alone.

Sometimes, you just have to ask for help. Not all problems can be solved by focus alone. There will be tasks that require a combination of 3 people working together.

When focus is not enough, then you probably need another hand to work on the project.

There's nothing wrong with asking for help.

The sooner you discover you need help; the sooner you try to find someone who can help you.

Action Guide:

Look at the projects that you are doing alone. Does it feel like it's getting next to impossible to finish them?

Then you probably need to ask for help.

Ask an employee for support or hire a freelancer to help you finish some aspects of the project.

Ask for help, then refocus on parts of the job you assigned to yourself.

25 - Drink a Green Juice First Thing in the Morning

What you put in your body has a big effect on how you think. On one hand, eat junk food first thing in the morning and you'll feel bloated and groggy all day. On the other hand, drink green juice in the morning and you'll feel energized instead.

There's obviously lots of recipes out there. You can even create your own if you want too.

However, most of these green juice (created or packaged) taste bad... Some are even AWFUL. "Yuck" as my younger brother used to say.

What I do is I drink a green powdered juice that I can easily prepare.

Out of all the brands that I've tried, I only found one that doesn't taste like crap.

The brand is called Organifi Juice.

Their website is:

https://www.organifishop.com/

Look, I know that I'm biased, but I suggest that you try making your own green juice first and then buy Organifi and compare it.

Trust me, it won't be as good when it comes to the taste (Organifi taste like candy). Plus, you don't have to spend time in preparation and cleaning your juicing machine.

Action Guide:

Drink your green juice first thing in the morning. You'll immediately see an increase in your focus and energy levels within 7-10 days of consistently drinking it every day.

26 - Should You Avoid Caffeine?

If you've been consuming strong caffeine (coffee, tea, anything with caffeine) every morning, then it would be hard for you to not drink one before every work day.

I understand your dilemma. I've been a coffee addict for years, and it took me a few months to even minimize it since the day I decided to stop drinking coffee.

The thing about caffeine is you can get dependent on it. It would feel like you absolutely need it (which you don't). That's why I recommend green juice in the last chapter, so you can stop being dependent on caffeine for your energy.

Caffeine also gives you that crash after the initial boost of energy. I'm usually super energized for 2-3 hours and BAM! I'm done, I can't focus, and I can't work properly anymore.

What You Can Do

Here are some of the things you can do to minimize and then eliminate your dependency on caffeine.

1 - Replace it with a better alternative (Water or Green Juice)

2 - Drink less by having smaller servings. If you drink 1 full cup of coffee, then serve a ¾ cup instead… then you change it to ½ after a few weeks… reduce it bit by bit until you kicked off the habit.

3 - Don't blame yourself for wanting to have some of it. For me, I don't mind having coffee at least twice a week. I don't really crave for it anymore since I started drinking water + green juice every morning.

4 - Go from strong to mild. Change the brand of the coffee you're drinking. Look at the caffeine level that you're consuming and change it from strong to mild.

5 - Do not go to the coffee aisle when you are grocery shopping. You cannot consume it if you don't buy it in the first place.

Action Guide:

Choose one idea (from the suggestions above) that you can apply today.

You can either start small or you can go "all in" if you have the willpower to stop consuming caffeine.

27 - Preserve Your Emotional Energy

We only have a limited amount of energy that we can spend all day. This includes our emotional energy.

Emotional energy is defined by our psychological capacity to express and manage our emotion.

We don't usually notice it but a lot of us are emotionally spent.

Do you feel like you don't want to talk to anyone anymore after an 8- hour work day? Do you wish Sally from the accounting department would just *shut up for a minute*? Do you feel like you're going to snap at any time?

If yes, then you are emotionally spent.

Your emotional energy is already drained.

That's why you need to recharge it… but how?

First of all, avoid time vampires. Time vampires' super-power is to siphon energy without you even noticing it. You'll just walk out of the conversation feeling like your battery just got drained.

Second, manage your emotions during high-stress work days. Do not get too attached to everything that's going right or wrong. Law of Murphy says that "whatever can go wrong, will go wrong." Remember that you do not have any control to everything that's going to happen. Stop stressing about it and think about the solution instead.

Third, physical work out every morning (if possible) is proven to lower stress, which helps you recharge your emotional battery and helps you gain more focus. If you can't do it in the morning, try to do it in the middle of the day. Just sneak in a 30-minute session in there… Your last option is to do it at night, 2 hours before you sleep.

Action Guide:

Identify the things that are siphoning your emotional energy. Ask yourself, are you managing your emotions well when it comes to those things?

How do you react whenever someone fails at the task that you gave them? Do you feel anxious, annoyed, and pissed off? Or do you feel calm, logical and reasonable?

Remember, focus on things that you can control. And most of the time, the only thing you have control over is the way you respond to certain situations.

28 - Say No and Mean It

Whenever we're dealing with time vampires, we tend to be too polite and say yes to their requests.

It's not that you want to say yes all the time. In fact, you know that you should say "no." But why do we keep saying yes when what we really mean is "no, I don't want to do it" or "no, I'm quite busy right now."

It's because we're afraid of conflict. We don't want people to feel bad or say bad things about us. So we become a "yes man or yes woman" and we gladly (or it appears on the outside) say yes to people's demand for our time and energy.

But this is a problem… and a big problem at that.

These distractions kill our focus and momentum. These distractions don't allow us to be the best version of ourselves.

So, you have to learn to say no…. And mean it!

Action Guide:

1 - Practice saying NO in the mirror. Seriously, just go in front of your mirror and say "NO" 30x-50x. Be comfortable in saying it. You're going to have to say no to a lot of things so you can say yes to the right things.

2 - Give "no" as an answer but give alternatives.

For example, someone wants "a minute of your time" but you really don't want them to always bother you this way.

What you can do is say no, and then explain why you're saying no.

It can go something like this:

"Hey Rob, I understand that you need help right now, but I'm going to have to say no. I'm very productive during 8-11am and I want to keep my momentum going forward. When it comes to these requests, I would really appreciate if you could ask them at least a day before the meeting or during the afternoon. Thanks, buddy."

It will seem weird or awkward at first to have to explain yourself, but you only have to do it once or twice. Once they are trained to accept your response, you'll now have less distraction and you just turned that time vampire into a productive friend.

29 - Say Yes, But Only If It Matches Your Goals

Now, you don't have to say no all the time as well!

You also have to say yes to new opportunities…. But only if it matches your goal.

Let's say that Sonny, VP of your company, wants you to meet a person coming over dinner at 7pm. If that guy can help you in your goals, then you should be open in canceling your original plan for the night. You should weigh the pros and cons of attending that dinner. You should know the consequences of your decisions.

So, say yes to opportunities, not all people who approach you are time vampires. Some will have the ability to help you in achieving your goals.

Action Guide:

What opportunity has shown up in your life recently? Make sure that you weigh the options of saying yes or no.

Is it really worth it missing your kid's soccer game while you attend an all-day meeting? Sometimes it's worth it and sometimes, it's not.

Learn to evaluate the situation and make a decision that you would stand for. Another thing to look at is the opportunity cost. You saying yes to one thing means you're saying no to another. Again, weigh your options. Choose the one that is more important to you, and stand by the decision you make.

30 - Exercise Every day

This is common knowledge. Exercise helps you become physically healthy, more energized, be happier, gain more focus, etc.

The problem is not about knowing how to exercise. The problem we have is in the discipline of implementation.

Most of us feel like we don't have the time to exercise.

With kids, our work, vacations, etc., there's just no way we can do it anymore, right?

But lots of people who are busy still manage to exercise every day or two. The key is to make it a part of your day. It's something you do like brushing your teeth or taking a shower.

What I suggest that you do is to start with a 15-minute workout routine. Most of us will have 15 minutes to spare, and it wouldn't really take too much out on our schedule.

There's a lot of 15-minute workouts that you can follow... seriously, just Google "15-minute workouts" and you'll find hundreds to choose from.

For your convenience, I put a sample 15-minute workout below that you can follow.

Action Guide:

Check out this link and follow the instructions. Working out, even for just 15 minutes will have a positive impact on your energy levels and your ability to focus.

Apply the strategy mentioned below:

https://www.self.com/story/a-15-minute-no-equipment-workout-thatll-sculpt-your-abs-and-arms

The 15-Minute No-Equipment Workout

- Plank to Dolphin
- Push-up

- Plank Tap
- Forearm Side Plank With Twist
- Bicycle Crunch
- Plank to Downward Dog
- Diamond Push-up
- Lateral Plank Walk
- Boat Pose

31 - Take Short Walks

Here's a list of famous people who took short walks every day...

- Aristotle. ...
- William Wordsworth. ...
- Charles Dickens. ...
- Henry David Thoreau. ...
- John Muir. ...
- Patrick Leigh Fermor. ...
- Soren Kierkegaard.

And there's a reason why they did it...

Walking outside helps you regain clarity. It helps in relaxing our minds and letting it wander for a bit.

Miraculously, lots of new ideas may come up during or after a walk. It's as if the walking part gives birth to new ideas hiding in the back of our minds.

Honestly, I don't even try to know the reason why that happens... I couldn't care less.

All I know is that when I take short walks (10-20 minutes) outside, I always come back refreshed and full of new ideas brewing in my mind.

Action Guide:

Walk outside your house or office after 2-3 hours of focused work. 10-15 minutes outside will help your mind to relax and be ready for the next task ahead.

32 - Run, Run, Run

When it comes to the physical benefits, running has the same effect as walking.

In addition to the physical benefits, it also helps you regain clarity and focus for the work ahead of you. But unlike walking, it's best to do running on a longer time frame to maximize its benefits.

Walking is best for gaining clarity, while running is for building energy and endurance.

When it comes to running, I recommend that you do it 3x-4x a week at 1 hour each session.

Also, run outside if you can. Running on treadmills is ok, but not as beneficial as having the full experience of seeing nature and feeling the different sensations of the outside world.

Action Guide:

1 - Go get your own running shoes from any of the famous brands. However, do not spend more than $120 for a pair.

https://www.esquire.com/uk/style/shoes/g24739613/best-mens-running-shoes/

2 - Get yourself a wireless earbud. It's best to have one that is specifically made for running. Listen to motivational speeches, lessons about a topic you're interested in or listen to your favorite music to make running more fun
https://www.cnet.com/topics/headphones/best-headphones/best-truly-wireless-headphones/

3 - Plan your route. There are free and paid *running app*s out there that you can use every session. Don't go crazy on the details, start with the free one if you're at the phase of just trying to build the running habit.

https://www.telegraph.co.uk/technology/mobile-app-reviews/10237554/top-10-running-apps.html

33 - Sleep Soundly

(Disclaimer, I am not a doctor and all I'm going to suggest in this chapter is based on my own experience. Consult your doctor before you do anything that I suggest here).

With that said, I'm passionate about sleep.

Why? Because I know its importance in my life.

My worst days has always been the ones when I didn't get enough sleep. Whenever I sleep less than 6 hours, the next day doesn't seem to blend well for me.

I just cannot function properly without 7-8 hours of sleep.

It's been rumored that Einstein slept for 10-12 hours a day.

We're no Einstein so 7-8 hours is enough for us.

I've tried many sleep optimizations over the years, some of them are useless and a waste of money and some worked well for me.

Action Guide:

Here are the strategies that worked like a charm for me:

1 - Total Darkness

I made my room super dark that almost no outside light goes through inside. This helps me tremendously in getting asleep fast.

2 - 5-HTP

I've tried many sleeping aids and this has the best effect for me. It also helps that it doesn't give me any migraine, morning grogginess or any side effects the morning after.

3 - No Device 2 Hours Before Sleeping

All the devices that we use nowadays emits light that signals the eyes that "it's still morning," that's why it's hard to sleep when you're still on your phone at night. Our brains get tricked by this harmful blue light, thus making it hard for us to get to sleep. This also affects our sleep as we don't get to have a deeper type of sleep whenever we use our devices too much.

4 - Earplugs

Outside noises may wake us up in the middle of our sleep. I found that a small earplug helps eliminate some of the outside noise I may hear while I'm asleep.

Choose a smaller cut because putting earplugs 8 hours every night may start to physically hurt your ears.

34 - Take Short Breaks

We are in a culture of Hustle.

When the celebrity entrepreneur, Gary Vaynerchuk said that we should hustle, I think a lot of people misunderstood what he meant.

When he said "hustle," he didn't mean that we should work 18 hours a day and sleep 4 hours at night. It's not about how many hours of sleep you have. It's about what you're doing during your waking hours.

The truth is, not all of us has the ability to work more than 12 hours a day. It's physically and mentally tiring to do on a daily basis... almost impossible for some.

What we can do is to maximize our time instead. Make ourselves more focused and more productive. Part of that is taking short breaks...

All the strategies I mentioned before has *taking a break* included in them. Why? Because it's as important as the work itself. So, don't be ashamed of taking a break from the *hustle*. We need it for us to stay effective and efficient. We need it so we can continue being at our best.

Action Guide:

Go back to all the strategies I mentioned before (time chunking, work chunking, Pomodoro, etc.). Are you implementing the "break" part or are you ignoring them?

35 - Start and Follow a Morning Routine

We are a creature of habits and routine. Not having our routines affects our circadian rhythms needed for us to stay healthy - emotionally, mentally and physically speaking.

If you're a writer, the most effective way to build a writing habit is to write at the same time every day...

If you're a basketball player, having a regular sleep schedule can help you maximize your talents...

Whatever your work is, you can maximize your effectiveness by having some kind of routine that you do every day.

I recommend that you start with a morning routine.

These are things that you do in the first 1-2 hours of your day. This morning routine helps you set your day up for success.

Most successful people have their own versions of morning routines. A combination of; drinking water or something healthy, journaling, meditation, exercise, and writing are the usual tasks.

If you want to learn more about morning routines, I recommend the book Miracle Morning by Hal Elrod.

Action Guide:

1 - Create your own morning routine. It could be 15 minutes, 30 minutes or pretty much whatever you want. The goal is to do something that will set the mood and energy for the rest of the day. If you start your day with something productive, you are more likely to keep the spirit of productivity and get more things done for the day.

2 - Research more about things that you can do on your morning routines. Not all of the things that we'll try will work for us. So, research more and find more things you can try.

36 - Take Naps

So, you've done most of the ideas in this book and you've become very productive. You're maximizing your time and you're very focused in your work. But there's just one big problem.

By the time the clock hits 12 at noon, you already feel tired and spent. You spent so much energy in the morning doing your important tasks, and you don't feel like working anymore.

You're just too tired already. So, what's the solution?

Simple: Take a 10 or 20-minute nap.

Taking a nap is proven to help you gain alertness and focus the easy way. Just rest your mind and body for a little bit, and you'll instantly get that power boost that you need so you can work from 1pm onwards.

Action Guide:

1 - Schedule your nap time during lunch. Make sure that you follow the same schedule every day, and nap at the same exact location as well.

2 - Expect the first week to be hard. You won't easily be able to fall asleep. I suggest that you set the timer for 25 minutes on your first week since the first 10-15 minutes will most likely be the time you spend trying to fall asleep. Then go back to the 10-20 minutes' timer as originally planned.

3 - Set a timer for 10-20 minutes. Sleeping more than 20 minutes can have a negative effect on you. You'll feel groggy and you won't be able to focus on your work anymore. So, trust me, stick with a 10-20 minutes' nap.

4 - Use an earplug so you don't have to hear other people's B.S. during lunch. I'm serious, there's way too much gossip going on during break time. Make sure you don't hear any of that.

37 - Stretch Yourself - Part 1

Go do a stretching exercise after every 30 minutes of work. Our body isn't made to sit all day. We're made to hunt and move. But there's obviously no need for that now.

So, we have to move our body constantly in order to stay in shape. One of the best ways to battle back pain and body aches is to do stretching exercises.

A 1-minute stretching session is all that you need for every 30 minutes of work.

It's crazy how a 1-minute stretching session can relieve you lots of stress in your body. Try it, it works!

Action Guide:

Find a place where you can do your stretching exercise. If you can't, there are many stretching exercises that you can still do at your desk.

If you're following the Pomodoro, then use a part of the rest time for stretching. Do this consistently throughout the day in order to build the habit.

Resources

Check out these simple stretching exercises you can do.

For people who have extra space:

https://www.shape.com/fitness/workouts/only-5-stretches-you-need

Stretching exercise in the office:

https://www.themuse.com/advice/17-desk-stretches-thatll-almost-replace-going-to-the-gym

38 - Stretch Yourself - Part 2

The last idea was about stretching yourself physically.

For this one, I'm talking about stretching yourself mentally. It's about stretching your capacity to think. To know that "you can do better" and to know that you have so much more potential in you.

Often, when we start something hard, we start to realize that we are capable of so much more. My friend always says "Big problems, big money," His point isn't just about the money. It's about expanding ourselves for what we can truly do. It's about evolving and being better than we were before.

So, this is my challenge to you.

CHOOSE TO STRETCH YOUR CAPABILITIES.

Are you thinking too small? Are you underestimating your capacity? This not only applies in your ability to focus but also in other aspects of your self-improvement journey.

Action Guide:

Do you really lack focus or you're just afraid of doing the work? Each of us has the ability to expand. Choose to improve every single day and learn to stretch your thinking cap.

Ask yourself, in what area of your life are you thinking too small?

39 - Note Taking Apps?

I've always been wary of using note taking apps.

I still use pencils and notebooks for most of my notes, so I'm kind of old school in that way. So, do you really need all these note taking apps? The answer is it depends.

If you're in a business that requires you to organize lots of information, then these apps may help you streamline the process.

However, if you have a simple business or a job that already has a system in place, then just use what you already have in the workplace.

Note: *Maybe a simple "Notes" app from Mac or PC's version of it will do*

You can also choose to use the free versions of different note taking apps so you can decide whether you need it or not.

Action Guide:

Read this review and choose the right one for you.

https://www.lifewire.com/best-note-taking-apps-4136590

Also, ask yourself if you really need a note taking app.

Do you take that many notes every day to actually need it?

Or a simple pen and paper will do?

40 - Review Your Day

In order to continue being productive, you have to make sure that your daily tasks are being done properly.

More than half of your task list will probably be the same on a daily basis. That means you can evaluate your daily tasks and find a way to optimize your time.

How can you make this task simpler? How can you maximize your working hours while doing these repetitive tasks?

Action Guide:

Take note of the time frame needed to finish certain tasks and find a way to finish them faster.

So how do you do that?

First, you have to look at the hours you need to finish them.

Second, identify the actions that needs to be done.

And third, find a way to get things done fast - by either working faster and coming up with solutions faster or by outsourcing the task itself.

41 - Review Your Week

During Saturdays or Sundays, I always do a recap of the work-week that I had.

Did I achieve my daily goals? How many tasks did I fail to do? How many pending tasks do I have to finish for the next work week?

Asking these questions, and taking notes, allows me to track my progress every week.

This helps me have a bigger picture of where I'm at in my journey.

Am I moving too slow? Am I inching closer to my goal?

I will not know the answer unless I'm tracking my weekly progress.

Action Guide:

Do a weekly review of your progress...

First, see if you're finishing the majority of your tasks on a daily basis.

Second, are you finishing the tasks that are actually getting you closer to your goals? Just because you're taking action doesn't mean you're getting closer to your main goals. You can't just *do the stuff*, you also have to *do the RIGHT stuff*

42 - Review Your Month and Year

Up next is your monthly and yearly reviews.

This is where you make a deeper evaluation of your goals.

You may be focus and productive, and you're getting things done... but you still have to see if you're moving towards your goals.

Your monthly and yearly reviews should focus on your results.

Are you getting sales? Are you making a profit?

This also applies to any endeavor. If you're in boxing, you could see if you improved your quickness. In songwriting, you can look at how many songs you've written. These aren't things that you can evaluate daily or weekly. These are the things that takes some time.

Action Guide:

Look at the bigger picture and see if you're taking the right steps toward your goals. If your goal is to make 100k per year and you only made 20k by July, then you're obviously off the tracks. It's time to evaluate your actions. It's time to evaluate what you're doing and achieving on a monthly basis because something is clearly not working. Identify the problem, then create a better solution so you can achieve your goal.

43 - Do Not Be a Perfectionist

I got lucky I guess. Early in my career, I decided that I'd rather have *speed of implementation* rather than *perfectionism.*

Being a perfectionist can be dangerous because nothing is inherently perfect. There will always be something better. There will always be an improvement to make.

In fact, Apple's billion-dollar strategy hinges on this exact type of thinking - that "nothing is perfect, **but we can still improve.**"

Look at all their products, they're pretty and simple to use. Lots of people buy them. Are they perfect? No. Are they the most feature packed? No.

What they do is they make upgrades every year and they don't focus on making the products perfect. Don't get me wrong, they are good products - but perfect? No.

As long as they keep improving every year, then Apple will continue to exist.

The Dangers of Perfectionism

1 - You Don't Get Things Done

Instead of moving to the next project, the perfectionist wastes his time away trying to make something perfect. Instead of testing the market's response, the perfectionist spends 5 years on a product that no one asked for!
Getting things done (as long as they are good) is better than getting things perfect.

2 - You Waste Something Good

In our quest to perfectionism, we tend to throw away "the good stuff" that we already made. *You spent so much time and energy on that thing and you're just going to scrap it?* No, you wouldn't.

Why don't you ask for other people's feedback first? Just because you don't think it's perfect doesn't mean no one will ever like it.

3 - You Become Delusional

To a perfectionist, nothing is ever good enough. People will try their damn hardest and a perfectionist will still see garbage.

You not only demean other people by doing this... You also make yourself paranoid. You start aiming for unwarranted requests and bad expectations.

"But Steve Jobs was a perfectionist" Yeah, and his employees hated him for this. Steve Jobs wasn't fun to be around with, he was not a person you would like to eat your dinner with. Also, Steve Jobs actually learned to lessen his perfectionism, this allowed Apple to tap into more mass-market (but still premium) products - which made apple grew.

Stop being a damn perfectionist. Unless it's life and death we're talking about, sometimes, good enough is good enough.

Action Guide:

Read this article about Steve Jobs.

https://www.inc.com/jeff-haden/chasing-steve-jobs-why-perfectionism-is-your-worst-enemy.html

Decide for yourself that you would focus on SPEED OF IMPLEMENTATION instead of perfectionism.

Just to be clear, I'm not saying that you should do crappy work.

No, you should always strive to produce a product or a service that **your intended audience will like.**

The keyword here is INTENDED AUDIENCE.

Someone who likes to read complicated books won't probably like my book. They'll complain about my grammar and my sentence structure. They will hate that I write as if I'm just talking to a friend. But he's not my intended audience so I couldn't care less. I would rather give awesome and actionable content that will change other people's lives than to spend thousands of hours making my writing sounds like somebody who I am not.

44 - Schedule Your "Pleasure Time"

I already touched on this a little bit on the other chapters, but this is important so I want to talk about it more.

Your pleasure time is important. It's something that you need mentally and physically. We all need a break from work and it's something that we should schedule as well.

Here are the possible things you can do during your break time.

YouTube, Facebook, Twitter, and Instagram

Social media is something that you and most people spend time on every day.

So, schedule your social media time. For example, you can use 7-8pm as your "social media time." You can also put a little bit of "Insta Time" during your working hours.

8am-10:30am can be work and then use 10:30-10:45 as your Insta time.

The point is to not use social media randomly. Make your social media time deliberate. Schedule it as if it's part of the work. I found this to be an effective way **to stop** checking my phone randomly throughout the day.

Other Habits (Entertainment, Sports, TV, Video Games)

These are mostly done during the weekends. Stuff like watching a series, a sports game, or any kind of fun activity.

Make sure that you schedule them on the weekends

Use this as an opportunity to recharge and forget about your work. When you're doing these activities, focus solely on the fun stuff you are doing... Turn off the notification and **stop checking your phone** every 10 minutes. Just focus on having fun so you can make these activities worth doing.

Action Guide:

Schedule your "Pleasure Time." Make them part of your weekly schedule and things to do.

By doing this, you'll enjoy your break time more, and you are more likely to be focused when you start working on your tasks.

45 - Learn to Disconnect

Our electronic devices have become an extension of our lives that it's almost impossible to not use them. But having that one day of break is a good reminder about what really matters in our lives.

Once a month (usually by the end of the month), I go to someplace close to nature and I disconnect from my normal world.

I don't bring the mac or the iPad. I still bring my phone but I put it on silent (and will only check it the next day).

I just disconnect from everything and everyone I'm familiar with. I go to some place where nobody knows me.

Normally, I just go for a swim, a meditation session, a massage, or I write (on a notebook) about ideas I want to implement in the near future.

This allowed me to renew my energy and enthusiasm for my work.

I recommend that you do the same and see if it'll have the same effect for you.

Action Guide:

Go find someplace near you where you can do the Disconnect Day. Do not bring any devices unless you really need to. Just do random stuff that you don't normally do. DOING NOTHING is perfectly fine! If that relaxes your mind, then, by all means, do nothing!

Other activities you can do are:
1 - Learning to draw
2 - Calligraphy
3 - Surfing
4 - Swimming
5 - Biking
6 - Rock climbing
7 - Trekking
8 - Going to a museum
9 - Spending the day on a library
10 - Going to a zoo

46 - Avoid Your Email

The majority of us open our email first thing in the morning. This is a problem because we're opening ourselves up to early distractions. An email is basically just a list of other people's agenda. If you get 20 emails a day, and you spend an average of 3 minutes per email, then you'll be spending an hour a day dealing with other people's agenda.

That's not very productive to do, especially in the morning.

So, if it's possible, and your work allows you to do it, avoid email as much as you can especially in the morning.

I only check my email twice a day.

Once at around 11am, and then once at 4pm.

Having the discipline to follow this routine will free up not only your time but also your mental load. Not having to think about too much stuff lets you focus on the task ahead.

Avoid your email and train people to notice your time frame. Better yet, let them know that you only check your email twice a day. Remember, **an email is just a list of other people's agenda**. Most emails don't need to have a reply. Choose the most important ones and stick to your schedule.

Action Guide:

Unsubscribe to the majority of your email subscriptions, except the necessary ones. Schedule your email time. Twice a day is plenty.

47 - Ask What the Process Requires

We get easily distracted when we don't know the next step in our task.

Let's say that you're a songwriter. When you run out of lyrics you can think of, then you suddenly open yourself up for distractions.

Not being prepared for this scenario can kill your focus and productivity.

So, you have to ask yourself what the process requires.

What can you do when these "lag" happens?
What can you do to make sure that you'll get back to work?

Let me give you another example.

Let's say that you're a Virtual Assistant for Real Estate Ads on Facebook. If your company is good, then you would have a list of script to use for every answer the customer may say.

Knowing these scripts is part of the process. In fact, it is the process. Knowing these answers is what the process requires.

So, you have to find a way to collect all the possible response from your customers and create a list of answers that you would say.

Whether you're in songwriting or Real Estate Facebook Ads, the point is to be ready in finding out a way to make the process seamless. The faster you find a solution, the less you are likely to give-in to distractions.

Action Guide:

Identify your most important tasks.

Ask yourself. "What are the aspects of these tasks that are more likely to have problems?"

Find those holes early in the process and find the best solutions you can think of.

This is not to say that you should look for problems that don't exist. No. This is about looking at the potential flaws of your project and being ready for what may happen because of those flaws.

48 - Work with Two Computer Monitors

If you've never had a 2-monitor setup before, then I guarantee you that you'll sing praise and hallelujah after you tried doing it.

Having that extra space of real estate allows you to open more tabs at the same time. This saves you time and energy in opening and closing tabs that you may use.

Having 2 monitors also allows you to view documents side by side. You can open one application for production and another one for research.

If you're a Facebook Ad Manager, you can open one side for the Facebook Ad itself, and then the other screen for your Facebook Page.

If you're a novelist, you can open one for Scrivener writing app, then the research materials for the other screen.

The possibilities are endless.

Don't worry if you're not super techie. There are lots of guides out there that you can use.

Just Google your computer model's name and add the word "dual monitor setup."

Action Guide:

Check out this article and find out what setup works for you.

https://www.lifewire.com/boost-productivity-with-a-second-monitor-2377817

https://www.pcworld.com/article/2057936/how-to-set-up-two-monitors.html

You don't have to be fancy with this. If all you can afford is the cheapest setup, then just go for it for now. Once you can already afford the more expensive ones, then go and upgrade to better monitors.

49 - Mindmap Your Ideas

Our brain has a hard time trying to make sense of all of our ideas at the same time.

So, whenever you have an idea for a project, I recommend that you create a brain dump via a mindmap. This allows you to put your idea into writing.

If you're coming up with a business plan, then create a mind map and just scatter all your ideas into one main theme.

It could potentially look like this:

Source: https://www.kub-uk.net/business-ideas-generate-sales/

The point here is to just do a brain dump and write whatever comes to your mind. Our goal is to get the idea out of your mind and into the screen.

This gives us a better understanding of what we can do next.

This also helps us in focusing on the right idea. *Does this idea have its own legs? Does it look like you have enough knowledge or experience to actually implement this idea?*

The mindmap gives us a better idea of what we know and what we don't know.

Action Guide:

Create a mindmap whenever an idea comes up. You always want to put the ideas into writing, and the best way to do that is to create a brain dump.

Do not judge your idea too quickly. Let it brew and take your time in assessing whether it's worth implementing or not.

I personally use MINDJET because I found the UI to be clean and easy in the eyes.

Check out your other options here:

https://www.slant.co/topics/1798/~best-mind-mapping-tools

50 - Increase Your Attention Span

Increasing your attention span can be a big factor on whether you'll be able to focus or not.

The good news is your attention span is elastic like a rubber. You can train yourself to focus more, to keep your attention on a specific thing or task.

But your attention span won't increase in itself, you have to take the time to actually work on it.

Action Guide:

Here are the things you can do to increase your attention span:

Keep It Quiet

Too much noise can distract us and put our attention on other things. Keep it quiet and work in a room where noise cannot get in.

I already suggested that you buy an earplug or a noise canceling headphone. I want to repeat it here because based on my experience, they are the most valuable purchase I had, related to increasing my focus and productivity.

Memorize Stuff

Practice memorizing cards so you can expand your mental alertness. Buy a set of playing card and practice memorizing by starting with 10 cards. Shuffle them and then look at it for a few seconds, then practice memorizing the order of the cards.

Stay Hydrated

A study at the University of Barcelona that a 2% decrease of water in our body has a huge effect on our mood and ability to focus. Always have water beside you and drink every 30 minutes or so.

51 - The Do Not Disturb Sign

It's crazy how effective this can be.

When you have a sign that says DO NOT DISTURB in your door, people seem to respect that and bother you less.

It won't completely eliminate time vampires but it will lessen the possibility of getting distracted.

Action Guide:

Buy a "Do Not Disturb "Sign. Preferably, a sign that you can flip just like the ones you see on stores.

52 - Create a NO TO-DO List

What you don't do can be as important as what you do.

You may feel productive and focused because you're getting things done, but are you actually doing the right things?

Are you actually getting closer to your goals?

Or are you just masquerading?

Are you just making a fool of yourself? Telling yourself that you're finishing tasks and "improving", even though in reality, you're not really moving towards your goals

Action Guide:

1 - Be honest with yourself. Identify the tasks that are actually getting you closer to your desired results.

2 - Identify your NOT TO DO list. These are the things that you shouldn't do or the things that you should outsource to other people instead.

53 - Ditch the Open Door Policy

Look, I know that management gurus are still recommending an open door policy for a lot of executives.

Please, stop...just stop!

It doesn't work for most organization because it creates a culture of distraction.

How do you expect the business to thrive if the CEO of the company gets distracted every 15 minutes?

How do you expect people to get things done if a new request comes in unexpectedly?

Action Guide:

Ditch the open door policy.

It's stupid and it sucks... sorry, there's just no other way to say it.

54 - Be Genuinely Interested in What You Do

Nothing beats passion when it comes to focus. Being interested in what you're doing gets you through the tough times.

When you're interested and committed to what you're doing, focus is easy. You don't have to fight your inner demons to be passionate about what you're working on.

Now, I cannot tell you what you should be interested in. It's something that you have to figure out for yourself.

Action Guide:

Find something you enjoy doing, outsource the rest if you can.

It may take you months or years, but finding out what you're good at and what you're interested in is already a worthy endeavor in itself.

Conclusion

Focus is the currency of the future, and it's something that we have in all of us. We just have to cultivate the habit and practice of eliminating distractions.

Focus - It's something that we have control over, and it's something that we can build.

Are there random distractions everywhere? Of course. But that's why we have tons of ideas in this book to fight them.

What I recommend is that you try some of the ideas in this book – and discard the ones that you think are silly.

Focus on the ones that work for you and keep adding habits that you know are helping you gain focus in whatever you're doing.

I wish you all the best in your journey to a more productive and focused life.

A Special Request

If you enjoyed reading this action-packed, daily guide, I would like to request you to leave a short book review on Amazon.

I understand that reviewing a book takes some of your time and I want you to know that I really appreciate you as a reader.

I treat each review as precious and I would really appreciate you taking the time of your day to leave one on the book's Amazon page.

Thanks for reading this book and I will see you on the next one.

OTHER BOOKS BY THE AUTHOR:

Check out the Author's Amazon Page:

https://www.amazon.com/AV-Mendez/e/B00XU2UW5S

or search for "AV Mendez" on the book category.

www.ingramcontent.com/pod-product-compliance
Lightning Source LLC
Chambersburg PA
CBHW031241050326
40690CB00007B/910